Ignite

Ambition

Author: Melissa Officer

Intro

How To...

Dear Reader,

You are the author of your story, and this guide was designed to include your truth. When you reach the questions throughout this book, be sure to challenge yourself to go beyond the surface with your answers.

Take your time and define what has brought you to this moment in your life and choose how you want to intentionally develop your future. I want you to be liberated from self-imposed limitations and I want to help propel you forward.

Ignite Ambition is a transformational guide created to uncover and evolve your potential. I use creative analogies to colorfully introduce each chapter and then I reveal the depths of my story that have enabled me to write this book.

Limitlessly pursue your greatness and ignite your ambition!

Internal Insight

Genuine Growth

Notable Navigation

Imaginative Ideas

Transformative Truths

Empowering Efforts

Excerpt

I realized my battleground raged on the terrain of my mind, and I was the only one with constant access to the front line. I had to accept the truth of my reality and grow from it, partnering with my fears while learning to trust myself. I've learned that life-altering revelations are often birthed on the back of adversity. - Pg 14

Copyright

Copyright © 2021 Melissa Officer
Published by Liberate You, LLC
All rights reserved.
Paperback: ISBN: 978-1-7351735-0-4
Ebook: ISBN: 978-1-7351735-1-1

Dedication

This book is dedicated to my mother Jessie Jones. I love you and I miss you. You believed in me and taught me to believe in myself. And in my heart, I will take you on this journey with me. I am overwhelmed by the thought of you. You were the embodiment of love and the depiction of joy and it was felt by all who knew you.

To my father, Michael Jones, thank you for working hard and teaching me to do the same. You've said that if someone else can do it, that means that I can too. You've been there for me, and I am grateful for all of the times that I was able to turn to you.

To my husband and friend Jayson Officer, our journey together has caused an evolution in the very core of who I am. You have been the catalyst that has caused my eyes to open and my soul to soar. It is because of you that I have been able to grow beyond the only reality I knew. I am eternally grateful that our paths are united. You are my partner and the love of my life.

To our fabulous four children, Hailey, Madison, Erin, and Joshua, live your absolute truth without permission or apology as long as it does no harm. As you discover your voice allow the world to hear it. Life is lived out on your level; it doesn't wait for you to become an adult. I believe in the power you possess, and I am honored to be your mother. Because of each of you, I am a better person. I love you all, and I am proud of you!

Ignite Ambition

CONTENTS

1	The Edge of Possible
2	Facing Fear
3	Powerful Defeat
4	Partnered Together
5	Developing Dreams
6	Breaking Free
7	Building Momentum
8	Grasping Growth
9	Caged Warrior

The Edge of Possible

Envision gliding out onto the icy glass surface of your future. With each gentle graze, your skates scratch the surface of the ice. Your anticipation is mounting as you envision your next move. Suddenly a shiver shoots down your spine as you realize the slightest wrong movement can pierce the core of your dreams, and if that happens, the ice below you will shatter as you plummet beneath the waters and your ambitions sink beneath the murky surface.

Like a deer in headlights, I have stood frozen in time with inaction incarcerating my moves. I didn't know how to push my goals forward, and I was afraid of making the wrong decision. I pictured my failed dreams disintegrating into obscurity, as the future "me" disappeared into the distance. Can you relate to this feeling? Have you ever chosen inaction to avoid the threat of the wrong action?

One of the most fearful places is the unknown. Here we stand in the vast possibilities of our current reality, daring to cross the threshold of our future to pursue a dream or desire. This unfamiliar territory can breed worry and wonderment, which can consume our consciousness and render us virtually immobile.

Nervously we can contemplate where our new pursuit is going to lead us. And a major hurdle that can separate us from our aspiration is our courage to believe that our ingrained desire is worthy of life.

Fear can be stifling and paralyzing. What if I'm wrong? What if I'm not good enough? What if I fail… miserably? These are just a few of my favorite fears, and I face them on a regular basis. I realize that my struggles are not based on my ability to succeed, although, if I'm sincere, sometimes I wonder if I'm the "right" Melissa Officer.

My biggest problems are that I judge myself, I ponder my failures, and I have a tendency to wallow in my defeats. For instance, for the last two years, I have wanted to take my biggest leap of faith and start my own company. I want to be instrumental in the evolution of self-empowerment. I want to be one of the voices of influence in people's lives, helping them to realize their possibilities and act on their ambition.

But then the voice of self-doubt would creep in, and it would hold my soul captive. But, instead of quitting on my intentions, I would simply distract myself by adding on to my list of goals. I would make my "big picture" bigger and think of all the new things I would now have to do. I didn't have to "quit" I just needed to give myself more time. I had to realize this was my way of avoiding the possibility of failure. After all, it's a lot harder to hit a moving target.

I decided to stop killing my dreams with doubt and silencing my souls desire. Then, I realized my goals were my gift's way of trying to live. I began to understand that the thing that made me worthy of my platform was simply the fact that I wanted it, and I would have to be the first one to notice my ability and make it happen.

We are all sitting on a gold mine of possibilities, but we can allow them to escape our focus because of the many excuses not to pursue something new.

If you are like me, then we have to be careful not to squander our opportunities for progress or fall prey to goal sucking apprehension. What if we realize that our mistakes can bring the greatest fuel for moving forward? And the pain from failure can develop depth in us if we can stay committed to the cause of our future. What if we could see our full potential?

All of our aspirations are impacted by one common purpose, one thread of design that starts in our minds. The truth is we are individually and collectively great. We have the power to define our perspectives and possibilities. As part of an infinite plan, we are meticulously designed and orchestrated for our purpose.

With absolute precision and forethought, we were intentionally created. It is not as if our parents conceived us, and then our purpose was decided. On the contrary, this world needs us and would be incomplete without our existence, so our parents conceived us.

Desire rings within the depths of who we are, but do we take advantage of the opportunity to answer and define the intuition within us? Have our goals been silenced by distractions, causing our ambitions to evade our focus?

Think about what your life would look like if you dared to attempt the "impossible." What if you could peel away every layer of excuse and reveal the depths of your desires? For just a moment, peer beyond your current reality and envision the future that calls to you.

Consider the direction you are moving in. Does it line up with your inner voice? If you can feel the desire for more pulling you forward, will you dare to begin a journey with me through this book? Together we will go on an internal scavenger hunt that will help define and develop our deepest desires. If ambition burns within your soul, are you willing to make sacrifices for it and pursue the things that ignite you?

What is your heart's DESIRE?

Find What You Love...
Then Opportunity Will Find You
- *Melissa Officer*

Time To Define

1. What makes you feel wanted/needed?

2. What makes you feel empowered/electric?

3. What makes you feel fulfilled/whole?

NOTES
(Whispering Thoughts)

QUOTE

"It's impossible," said pride.
"It's risky," said experience.
"It's pointless," said reason.
"Give it a try," whispered the heart.

- Anonymous

Facing Fear

I know the feeling of unyielding gripping fear. The type of trial that makes your heartbeat quicken when you think about it. It's the deep ache in the pit of your soul that makes your chest cave while anxiety consumes your thoughts. Imagine the darkness of fear hiding deep in the shadows. It leers maliciously, licking its fangs, as it eagerly anticipates the next bite from our consciousness. It feeds on our thoughts, and it can consume our minds. The darkest places in life will devour us if we surrender to the shadows that surround our souls.

Fear's stealthy nature will oftentimes change its appearance so it can go unnoticed in our lives as it awaits the perfect opportunity to raise its daunting head. For instance, I battled with the fear that my family and the world would be better off without me. I felt worthless because I thought I wasn't good enough.

I lived my life devoted to my faith, regularly attending church services six days per week. I was in the choir, on the praise team, a praise service leader, teacher, and facilitator, but that didn't silence my internal pain. And it felt like a consuming contradiction, that while I was immersed in the church, I was contemplating suicide.

I believed my faith would deliver me, and at times I felt relief and joy, but I also faced darkness and judgment. I felt the constant burden of pursuing perfection, and I consistently worried about failing. I was taught to believe that I was a sinner, and the only way I could find any good in me was through a savior. I was desperate to find forgiveness for my humanity.

I became dependant on validation as I sought approval from others and focused on making them happy. I strived to be the perfect wife, mom, daughter, sister, and church member, attempting to fulfill people's expectations of me. And when I failed, I devalued my worth. I didn't realize I had built a foundation of codependency, and I needed to restructure my beliefs.

How did I get to the point of believing everyone would benefit from my absence? It started with a simple lie I told myself, "I'm not good enough." A lie that began to grow, and with snowball like momentum, it began to consume me, and I believed all of my family's struggles were somehow my fault.

Years ago, my husband and I struggled financially with one income and four small children. Our bills were always playing a game of hide and seek, choosing to pay the one closest to disconnection while the other bills hid out of sight. Until one day, our house of cards began to fall. We received a letter from the sheriff's office with a notice to vacate and an auction date set for our home. I came face to face with the fear of losing our home. We scrambled to find a way to stay.

We were able to get on a repayment program that bled us financially dry. There were times we had to choose between diapers and food. There were times our electricity was disconnected and water too. We went through a winter without heat and a summer without air conditioning. Because we didn't have enough, I felt I wasn't enough. I felt like everything was my fault, and at any moment we could lose it all. I was terrified.

Once we were able to get passed those financial hardships, I still felt like a failure. I didn't realize that I had given myself permission to devalue myself. Our internal conversation is the one that is loudest in our lives. Regardless of what anyone says to us, it is what we tell ourselves that has the deepest impact.

My fear has many faces. I see it in the struggles of marriage, and the times we battled with mutual infidelity and faced the brink of divorce. I see it in the loss of trust and the fight to stay together. I see it in raising four children and hoping that I'm present enough to impact their lives and distant enough for them to find their own path. I see the face of fear when I think about living the rest of my life without my mom and accepting the brutal reality that she died from cancer, and she really isn't coming back. I see it in the mirror when I feel inadequate. And I see it when I dare to change my reality and reach beyond what I've always known. I had to face my fears.

Our lives are characterized by the choices we make. When we are confronted with life-altering circumstances, will we shrink away from the seemingly impossible, or will we be unstoppable and control the fear that tries to incarcerate us?

These breath wrenching moments are the times that cause our faith to tremble; they cause our confidence to violently shake. Moments like these bring us to our knees, and while we hang in the balance, we have a decision to make. This time will we cower in defeat, or will we allow the conqueror within us to rise up and change who we are? These challenges define us, but what does this mean? How can we defend ourselves against fear when it is an invisible, shape-shifting invader?

> "No one can make you feel inferior without your consent."
>
> - Eleanor Roosevelt

Our solutions for progress will be as varied as our lives and circumstances. But a rival that we all seem to confront is fear. What if instead of trying to defeat it, we exposed and revealed the vulnerability that resides within it? It can't survive without us, and we can't live without it.

I realized my battleground raged on the terrain of my mind, and I was the only one with constant access to the front line. I had to accept the truth of my reality and grow from it, partnering with my fears while learning to trust myself. I've learned that life-altering revelations are often birthed on the back of adversity.

Adversity doesn't come to destroy us; it comes to develop depth within us. Through our tears and struggles, we learn about ourselves. We discover how to evolve and exist independently from the ideal picture of what we thought life should look like.

We can focus on what "is" instead of what "was" or the negative what "ifs." Will we choose to allow a mental transformation to take place so it can change and redefine our direction as we pursue our next reality?

> Don't run from fear; learn to walk in tandem with it!
> - Melissa Officer

Once we are aware of the fear that lives within us, we can dominate our doubt and subdue our scared nature. We can harness our fear and face it. And instead of allowing it to inhibit us, we can choose to walk in tandem with it as we define its limit.

Potential is beating within all of our souls. The thud of each gripping moment is challenging us to stand at the threshold of time and welcome the newness of "next." Some of us have faced seemingly insurmountable odds, yet we have arrived at this moment of opportunity, and it's beckoning us to greatness. It's time for fear to bow down and allow progress to be pursued. Are you anything like me? Can you hear the call for expansion ringing in your ears? Are you provoked to answer your quiet call for more?

This is the moment, your moment, and my moment where we can stare fear in the face and stand toe to toe. Where the flutter we now feel in our chest, is that of high expectation and confidence instead of consuming doubt. Imagine pacing the floor with anticipation, watching the clock wind down on our current reality.

The ultimate climax is about to be revealed. There is an exact moment where life will publicize our inevitable success, although it has been riddled with fear, failure, and defeat. Now is our opportunity to embrace all of life's tragedies and triumphs as the culmination of who we are today. Let's own our truth.

Time To Define

1. What fears do you need to face?

2. Has your fear changed appearances, if so, how?

3. How did your darkest moments change you?

NOTES
(Whispering Thoughts)

> ## QUOTE
> **F.E.A.R.**
> has two meanings:
> Forget Everything And Run
> - OR -
> Face Everything And Rise
>
> -Zig Ziglar

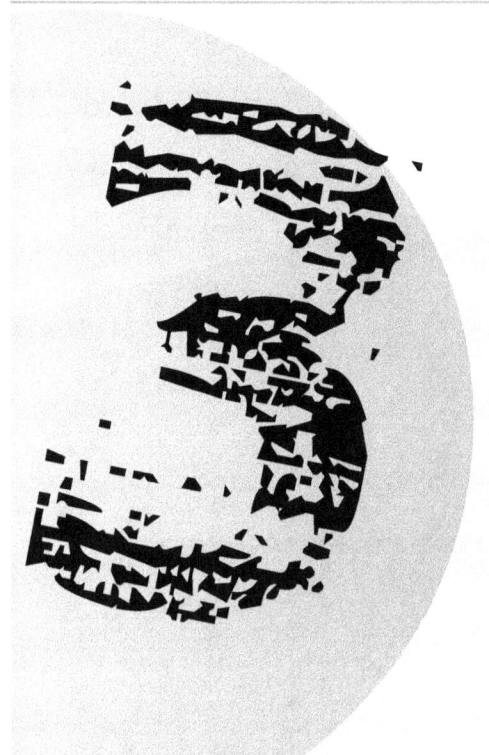

Powerful Defeat

Defeat can transform into power after it goes through a process of evolution. At times I've imagined my failures as if they were a story playing out on a screen. There I am alone, abandoned, filthy, and cold. My clothes are worn and torn. I'm in the midst of utter desolation. Some of it I caused, the rest of it happened to me. It's dark. My spirit is crushed. My heart is broken. There is no hope, nothing left, only an existence consumed by wasted ruin. Tears run through the dirt on my face. Gradually I lift my head and look up, with pain resonating from my countenance. My body shakes from sobbing. I don't know how I got to this place of devastation.

It is as if the tragedies of life surrounded me, and I've been swept away by the current of pain. I long to repair the damage that I see in my life, but each stone I touch is unmovable, and every chasm is impassable. Frantically I try to fix my mistakes, but nothing will change. Exhausted, I finally realize that my efforts are futile, and every part of my history is permanent. The only thing that can free me from my mental incarceration is a change in my perception. I had to face and accept that my past details helped sculpt my reality. The chaos of failure, depression, and self-hatred have created a facet of me that would not have otherwise existed. I've learned to honor the process that produced me. And I respect the courage it takes to realize this truth.

Our struggles can be used to validate our voice in someone's life and our own. Every excruciating internal scar has caused us to become who we are. And there is an undeniable beauty that evolves from the ugliness of life.

For instance, the lingering fear from almost losing our home evolved into fighting for our financial increase and focus. We discovered ways to learn about money management and grow financially.

And recovering from infidelity has redefined the way that I love and my view of faithfulness. The vicious cycle of retaliation didn't cause growth or healing. It caused distance and fear, and for a time it weakened our relationship. The pain and fear I faced during our struggle reshaped my reality and my willingness to be naively vulnerable. And in time, it helped empower me to see my value and worth in a different light.

Jayson and I were married at the age of twenty-two, and we were both virgins and very religious. We had never smoked or drank alcohol, we didn't go to movie theaters, I didn't wear pants, make-up, or jewelry, and the list of don'ts continued. We followed the "rules", and we were monogamous in our marriage for fifteen years.

The reasons we were unfaithful are very different, but they are both rooted in a place of hurt. At times it felt nearly impossible for us to stay together after broken trust. We had to find the strength to grow and realize the value that still exists in each other and our relationship. We had to learn to love again.

We have healed in our own ways and found our value and worth as individuals, discovering that when we know who we are and what we want individually, then we can find wholeness together. Our relationship is stronger now than it has ever been. We have grown and evolved together, we enjoy spending time together and are in love with each other. Although we will never be able to erase the past we have learned to grow from it.

Evolving as a mother has caused me to realize that being a good parent means I grow from my mistakes, and there isn't a definition of right parenting. There is, however, a definition of wholeness for our family. Being whole doesn't mean I have to sacrifice everything that I want and only make them happy. Being whole means, we've learned how to heal after I've hurt their feelings or they've hurt mine. Being whole relies solely on the opinion of our household. It is an individual relationship with each of our children. It is the validation of their voice and realizing that life is on their level, and their issues are as important as mine. We learn from our children, and they learn from us. And we have the strength to empower them on their level of life.

I attribute much of who I am as a mother to my mom; she is the example I still follow to this day. When she passed away, it consumed me. It felt like I couldn't breathe, I couldn't think, nothing seemed real. I had never felt that type of pain before, and I needed her to console me. I wanted to cry out to her and run into her arms. I wanted to weep in her lap while she stroked my hair and told me it would be okay, but I couldn't. She was the one I talked to when life was hard, and I didn't know what to do. She listened to me, guided me, and wanted the best for me. She helped sculpt the core of who I am with love, compassion, and concern. She taught me how to get up and keep moving forward. And now that she was gone, I'd have to face this unimaginable pain without her. When I felt the pain of losing her would consume me, I would hear her voice telling me I'll be strong enough to bear it. When I sobbed until I shook, I could feel her presence. My mother helped give me life, and a part of her DNA still flows through me, and she will always be with me. My mother empowered me to be able to cope with her death by the life that she lived and all that she instilled in me. And she still gives me strength.

We were all created with willful intent, and we are all part of a collective journey. Our triumphant individual stories are intermingled with the brutal details of our pain and defeat. We need our success and failure to grow and evolve into the future version of ourselves that will be revealed.

No matter how different our stories are, they can unite us. When we struggle or succeed, it illustrates our commonality with the people around us. When we keep moving forward, our beautiful imperfections show our strength and movement despite our challenges.

If at times, we feel insufficient for our next phase of life, we can pull from the power that has already developed within us. We don't have to allow insecurities and excuses to grow in the place where greatness wants to reside. Imagine the power we'd possess from realizing that the idea of flawlessness is a flawed concept and, at times, superficiality can skew our view of reality.

We don't have to be invincible, unstoppable, or impossible to match. Like a warrior, we can face the battle raging within our minds. We have limitless power to change our lives if, instead of being haunted by our past, we chose to be empowered by it.

Our lives are not mystery novels. We get to write our story with each decision we make. Why should perfection be our pursuit when there are so many details in our flaws? Instead of hating or devaluing our past, we can realize the evolution that has developed in us because of our experiences.

Time To Define

1. What experience with defeat can you use to fuel your future?

2. What is the greatest power that you possess?

3. How will you use your power to provoke movement in your life?

NOTES
(Whispering Thoughts)

QUOTE

"I can be changed by what happens to me. But I refuse to be reduced by it."
Maya Angelou

Partnered Together

The translucent shadows of our lives glimpse each other like peering into a cloudy mirror. If we begin to remove the debris that is obstructing our view, we can start to see the things that relate us all.

Then with each revealing gaze, our differences can be overshadowed by our similarities. When we allow ourselves to share our stories while being defenseless and honest, it can form a genuine bond with those around us. Have you ever met someone, and in some ways, their story mirrors yours?

Not all of the details are the same, but you can feel the closeness of your encounter. If the timing is right, an emotional bond can grow with little effort. Typically it can take years to form deep connections, but if you have common ground with someone, it can bridge the gap of time.

Our experiences give us the power to provoke and encourage each other. Success is strong enough to stand alone, so it is easy for us to share those stories. However, the feebleness of pain produces the need for a partner.

We need the strength of one another and the power of determination to overcome the collateral damage of pain. We can then realize that our past allows us the ability to relate to each other in ways that transcend words.

I have had the privilege to partner with different individuals during very trying times in their lives. In most cases, we didn't have a close relationship before their tragedy or circumstances arose. In the midst of their chaos, they allowed me to be there for them, and our connection began to grow.

I shared some of my past heartbreaks with them, and I openly heard their voice. And in exchange, they let their guard down and engaged in an opportunity for an emotional release.

When we allow our hearts to break and tears to flow, we are actually giving our souls permission to "let go." When we are there for each other, it develops a level of comfort and strength that we may not have found on our own.

I finally realize the depth of power that comes from having a partner in different areas of my life. Because we don't all face the same experiences we don't relate to everyone in the same way.

My relationships have developed like dipping my toe into the water before jumping into a pool. My friends and I have gradually built our relationships as we discovered our commonalities. I realized that I didn't have to hide behind a smile or pretend everything was okay. I could let my guard down and reveal the deepest parts of me and what lies beneath my surface. As my inner circle began to grow, I discovered that each connection was unique. One person didn't reflect every facet of my journey, and I needed them all to help me grow, develop, and see the possibilities along the way. I am better because I have them and I hope they're better because they have me.

'To be yourself in a world that is constantly trying to make you something else is the greatest accomplishment."

-Ralph Waldo Emerson

Our experiences are not just for us. Tribulation, as daunting as it is, does not come to have an isolated impact. The lessons it brings are not intended to be concealed within one heart; they are meant to be given out. Our stories are our legacy of greatness.

If we camouflage our struggles instead of revealing them, that will diminish the reach of our influence. We are connected through our experiences. Although our struggles are individual, they can unite us. To help each other survive, we must be willing to be emotionally raw. We can build a level of trust that will allow us to be vulnerably honest with each other.

Life is filled with uncertainty and unfamiliar territory, but we can discover how to move forward, one day at a time, and one pain at a time. Don't run from where you come from; nothing is more relatable than common ground.

Time To Define

1. What life experiences give you common ground with others?

2. How can you help someone to heal?

3. If you are hurting, will you share your pain?

NOTES
(Whispering Thoughts)

> **QUOTE**
>
> Be strong enough to stand alone, smart enough to know when you need help, and brave enough to ask for it.
>
> - Ziad L. Abdelnour

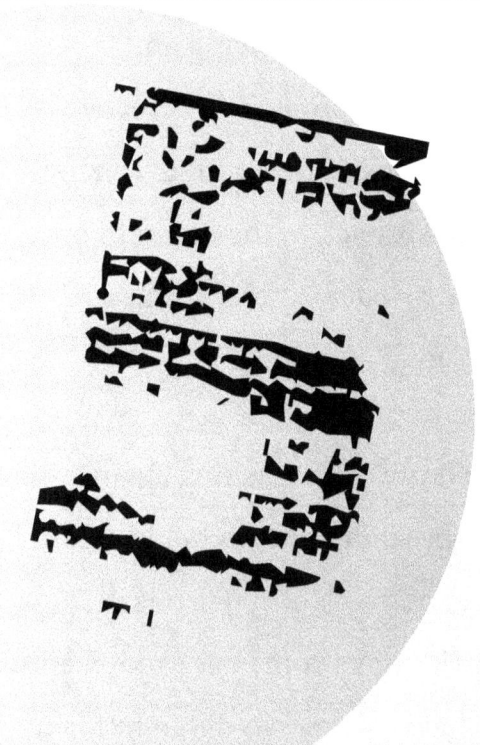

Developing Dreams

The crashing waves strike against the shore as if they are in a race to reach the finish line. Before the victor can be determined, the pull of the tide causes the waves to retreat. Then with magnificent force, the ocean rushes in again. How can the magnitude of the ocean be contained?

The water in the ocean is continually evolving and becoming something new. The ocean evaporates and creates clouds. Then rain, snow, or hail fall back to the earth to join our lakes and rivers; eventually, it all leads back to the ocean to once again crash against the shores. These waters stretch as far as possible to fulfill their continuous evolution.

Every day we give out into our world, crashing against the shores of life. Every contribution, great or small, is being cycled through our society. We are pieces of a collaborative puzzle, and eventually, our outward contributions come back to benefit us. And when they do, they may have taken on a different form than what we gave out.

This persistent cycle also lives within our thoughts. Our minds are given the opportunity for constant evolution. We are presented with glimpses of ideas that are waiting for the chance to grow and to become something new. Are we willing to feed our full potential into this world by giving our future the time and attention it needs?

It can be challenging to believe in a new idea when we don't know how to make it grow. One day I decided that I should at least try; otherwise years from now I would find myself saying "I always wanted to _____ but I never did".

For years I wanted to be an author and speaker, but I was unsure of how to accomplish either. I had no connections or opportunities, only a dream that whispered deep in my soul. I knew that I was created to connect with people and encourage them to realize their dormant greatness, but I was nervous and unsure of how to move forward. I stopped making excuses and started making a plan. I grafted speeches and spoke to invisible audiences. I consistently wrote, although I was unsure what book I was creating.

I began to believe my dreams were possible before anyone knew my name or desire. I validated my voice and my choice to bet on me!

I began to look for small, reachable opportunities to develop my platforms so that I could create space for my voice. I spoke at schools and started a Youtube channel. I realized that if I began to build on my desires slowly, then opportunity would have to come and meet me on my level.

Every small step began to feed my belief that my goals were possible. I realized that while I worked on my focus, my confidence began to grow. I allowed myself to see the "me" that I was becoming.

By feeding our potential, we are equipping our future selves to be greater than our current reality. Our success is the result of working towards a goal even when we can't see the finish line. By making guidelines towards our target, we can move forward with willful intent, as we stay focused on the grandeur of our potential greatness.

The influences we surround ourselves with impact what we believe to be possible. When we expose ourselves to the environment we want to thrive in, then it can help us grow more rapidly in that direction.

We will become surrounded by opportunity when we dive deeper into developing our longing desires! When we allow ourselves to be submerged in our intentional dreams, there will be waves of thoughts that will show us ways to fulfill our goals. We can also gain momentum by following the example laid out by people who have gone before us.

In the journey of defining our truths, we can develop the tools needed to grow past our current reality. There will be obstacles along the way, and it is up to us to allow our timeline and goal line to bend and fit within the challenges we face. If we get stalled along the way, we must never give up on our intentions.

Opportunities will become evident when we release our doubts and push forward towards the newness of next. We can work on the things that reflect our internal desires as we dedicate the time we have now to our future.

Look back to chapter one, what makes you feel empowered and fulfilled? Allow those desires to be worthy of your time. Have you taken the time to define the center focus of your intentions? You can continue to develop your direction by establishing the individual steps needed for accomplishment.

Time To Define

1. What is your ultimate desire?

2. What connections do you want to create?

3. How can you prepare for your future?

-

NOTES
(Whispering Thoughts)

> ## QUOTE
> Start where you, with what you have. Make something of it and never be satisfied
>
> - George Washington Carver

Breaking Free

Imagine being lost in a house of mirrors. The distorted panes of glass confuse your path, making it virtually impossible for you to escape. With each winding turn, you're faced with a new obstacle to overcome. Some reflections reveal a skewed view of you. And at times, your steps cause you to collide with the mirrored glass in your path. What looks like a way of escape can actually be a reflection of what's behind you. If you make the wrong move, it can take you deeper into the maze instead of leading you out. You can feel your anxiety growing. You are beginning to feel stuck in a box as you search for clues to help you escape.

We can find ourselves confined to levels of life, closed within reflective walls vigorously trying to escape. Some of our paths can seem to lead us further away from our goals. Relentlessly, we try a new direction but, we can be unsure of which way to turn. Which path will set us free?

Being stuck in a redundant cycle can be stifling, reliving what seems to be the same day, over and over again. If things are remaining the same and no freedom can be found, perhaps we are moving in the wrong direction. How can we escape the box that we have grown accustomed to and finally grasp the goals that have evaded us for too long?

Think about the change you want to see or where you want to go next. Is your current routine merely fulfilling life's obligations, or does it include time for your deepest desires? Are you satisfied with where you are? And if not, what do you specifically want to change?

When we know the motives behind our movements, then we are more likely to harness and protect our time. And this realization can enable us to accomplish the "more" we are looking for in our world. It will also give us the foresight to decide what is worthy of our time and help us to work towards our heart's desires.

Because I realize that time is our greatest commodity and that we cannot replenish it, I can be obsessive-compulsive when it comes to making a schedule. At one point, I had created schedules for myself and our children I offered to make my husband one as well, surprisingly, he declined, and kids aren't interested in time management (sigh). My life comes with a host of commitments, namely Jayson (my husband), Hailey, Madison, Erin, Joshua, our two dogs Max and Kodi, a full-time job, and the dreamer that lives within me.

Sometimes I can't stay on task, and I need my planner to help me remember what I was supposed to be doing. I use it as a tool to track my gradual progress and accomplishments.

Schedules are a way to monopolize on the moments that are given to us. It is an illustration of the direction we are moving in, and it can reveal opportunities for us to escape the mundane.

When we define our schedule, we can incorporate time to focus on our goals. We can accomplish our commitments and still have the opportunity to grow towards self-discovery and fulfillment. When we plan out our day, it can help slow the chaotic whirlwind of life. We can align ourselves with our desires and forward focus. A schedule can also give us space to have measurable time set aside for the things we enjoy.

When you create a schedule, be sure to include time for yourself and the things that bring you happiness. By examining our days, we can discover hidden moments of freedom and decide where we have time for the things that matter most to us.

If a schedule feels incarcerating to you and you can't fathom putting your time into boxes, then don't! Use this space to create a list and choose an ideal time for you to work on one goal. Allow your start time to fluctuate and set a timer daily, for at least one hour, and commit to working on your goals.

Sometimes I have to use my schedule as a guideline instead of my timeline. I focus on accomplishing 1 -3 things for the day and, I squeeze them in where I can; all that truly matters is that it gets done.

My Ideal Schedule

(Things don't always go as planned)

Night/Overnight	Early Morning
10:30pm - 5:00am Sleep	**5:00 - 6:00** Music, Shower, Get Dressed, Connect Within **6:00 - 6:50** Journal/Social Media Prep/Define My Voice/Goal Focus **6:50 - 7:30** Kids Up/Get Ready to Leave **7:30 - 8:00** Commute: Record Thoughts, Listen to Audio Book or Motivational Speeches
Daytime	**Evening**
8:00 - 5:00 Work & Commute At work make small movements from the sidelines Set 1 goal to accomplish on breaks, lunch, or downtime (relaxation counts!) ***Weekends 7:30 - 11:30 = Goal Domination ***	**5:00 - 6:45** Workout/Go For A Walk/Family **6:45 - 7:45** Family Time/Dinner/Clean up **7:45 - 8:45** Goal Development **8:45 - 9:30** Time w/Jayson **9:30 - 10:00** Shower/Prep Tomorrow **9:30 - 10:30** Relax/Bed Time

Your Schedule

Night/Overnight	Early Morning

Daytime	Evening

Where does the time go? Reality can paint a different picture than what we planned.

In the pages to come, you can track your day to day reality. This can help you adjust your schedule and set realistic expectations for your time.

Once we know where our time is actually going, then we can redirect its flow and align with the current of our desires.

Let's put our lives into a simple math problem. Use the following guide to subtract your commitments from the 24 hours we are each given. As you move down the guide, subtract from your reduced remaining time.

My Week Day

24 Hours	The Details
-7	Sleep
17	**REMAINING**
-1	Shower/Dress/Meditate/etc.
16	**REMAINING**
-1	Kids up/Pack Lunch/Get Ready
15	**REMAINING**
-9.5	Work & Commute
5.5	**REMAINING**
-.5	Unwind from work
5	**REMAINING**
-1.5	Make/Eat Dinner as Family Homework Help
3.5	**REMAINING**
-1	Time with Husband
2.5	**Goal Focus/Plan tomorrow**
+3	Room To Grow

Work Your Magic

24 Hours	Your Details

Record Reality

(Things don't always go as planned)

24 Hours	Your Details

Record Reality

(What actually happens to your time?)

24 Hours	Your Details

Record Reality

(Set realistic expectations for your day)

24 Hours	Your Details

NOTES
(Whispering Thoughts)

> **QUOTE**
> If you talk about it, it's a dream, if you envision it, it's possible, but if you schedule it, it's real.
> - Tony Robbins

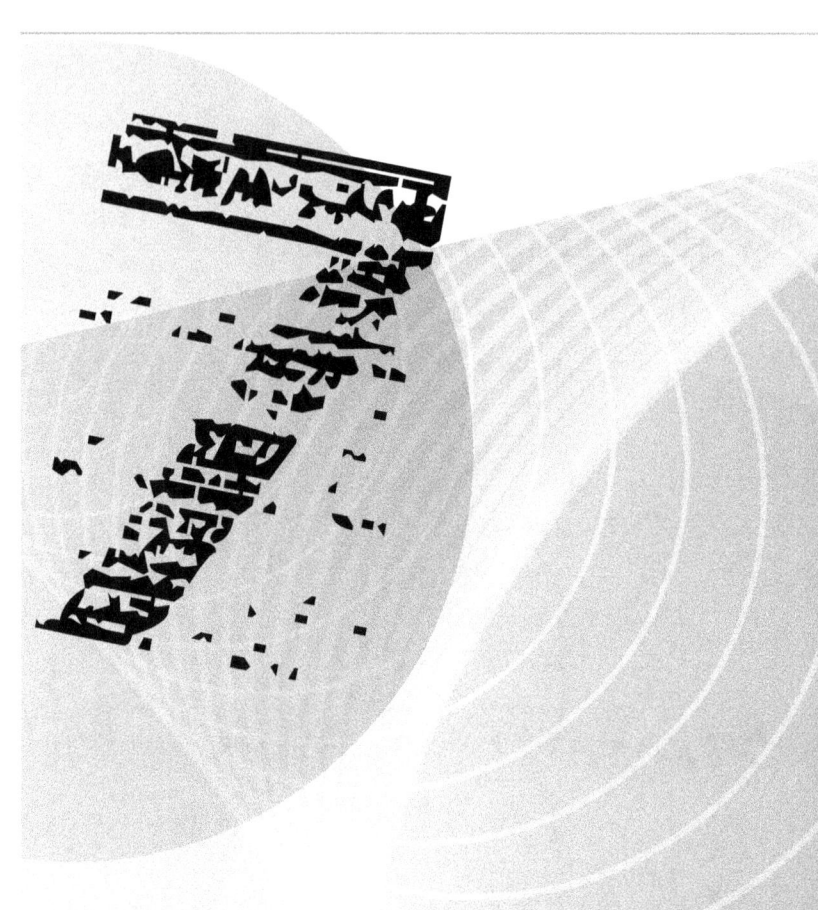

Building Momentum

Imagine the high pitched squeal of a swing set. You are sitting perfectly centered in the firm and flexible rubber seat. With anticipation, you hold onto the chains as you walk your feet back until your toes can barely reach the ground.

Then you lift your feet and allow the inertia from your body weight to push you forward. You kick your feet out in front of you and then you pull them back in, over and over again you push and pull your body through the air as you begin to climb higher into the sky.

Soon you reach the point where the swing set can't go any higher, and you realize the only thing that will allow your excitement to reach its pinnacle is to let go, jump off and fly. Your heart is racing; you are afraid and excited at the same time. Adrenaline is coursing through your body, it takes over, and suddenly you let go of the only thing holding you back, and you soar through the air.

Life can be like the back and forth motion of the swing. Typically we start our days at a slow pace, gradually increasing our speed just enough to accomplish our obligations. Once our needs have been met, instead of reaching our pinnacle, many of us slow our movements down and allow our feet to scrape the ground until we reach an anticlimactic stop. Then we get up the next day and repeat the same routine with no lasting escape from the mundane. What if we decide to gradually build towards a goal that would help us feel the exhilaration of fulfillment?

What we focus on becomes our reality, and we get to determine our direction every day. Allow your goals and ideas to become tangible by having a daily objective. For us to reach our destination, we have to know where we are going. Next, we are going to develop a path to achieve notable changes in our lives.

Start by choosing three huge goals for the year, not the beginning of the year, the next twelve months starting now. I use my birthday as my year marker instead of January 1st because it has more value to me. I'm more likely to accomplish a goal before my next birthday than I am to stay focused on a new year's resolution. And it's easier for me to work towards a date in front of me than remember my goals from a date that is behind me.

We get to decide the details that will enable us to move beyond our current reality. Every day we have the opportunity to push ourselves forward and surrender to the pull from our internal desires. We get to uniquely define our goals and decide the path in life that will bring us the most satisfaction.

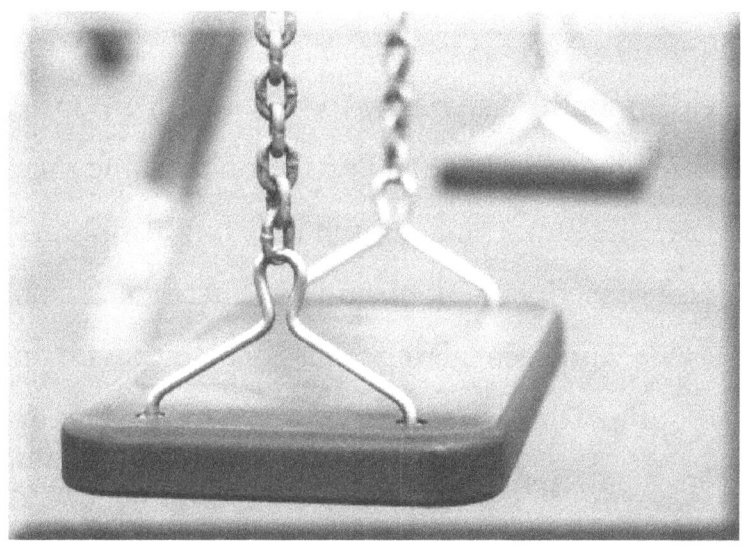

Similar to being in a game of follow the leader find someone who is living out a mirror image of your ambition. And follow their example instead of creating all of your steps from scratch. Then add your details to develop what you want your path to look like. If we view the people on our same path as partners instead of competitors, then we can learn from their example while producing our own.

Try approaching your three goals in four-month segments. In your first four months, decide the foundation you want to build on. Decide where you want to be four months from now and map it back to a starting point. Choose your first focal point and be sure it is specific and includes why you want it and how you will get it. Use as many details as possible. For instance, if you want to grow by 100 social media followers in four months to help establish your voice, realize that's 25 people per month. Watch how-to videos, join groups, Tell someone about your page and while you're telling them about it, simply ask them if you can pull it up on their phone and then click subscribe for them and say "there you go, now we're connected!" and keep talking. That's one down with only 24 to go for your first-month focus. Growth is gradual, so be sure to stay consistent. In the pages to come, you will find space to map out your focus in four-month increments. Set your intentions and search the internet to see what steps are already out there to help guide your path.

If at the end of four months, your first goal is complete, then celebrate! Make it a big deal and fuel your fire to keep moving forward.

After you celebrate, begin your next step towards fulfillment. If you didn't reach your goal, honor the steps you have taken and the fact that you have intentional focus. Recommit yourself to your heart's desire and stay focused on your first goal. You are not out of time, remember, time is on your side. Whatever your goals are, Decide, Define, and Develop them!

Time To Define

1. What are your three focal points for the next twelve months?

    -

    -

    -

2. Why are these three goals important to you?

3. What is your starting point for each goal?

NOTES
(Whispering Thoughts)

QUOTE

It isn't where you come from; it's where you're going that counts.

Ella Fitzgerald

Goal # 1

Example Page

Decide What: Side Photography Business

Define Why: Express creativity, enjoyment, extra income

Brainstorm Boxes

What type of photography	How do I start
- Weddings - High School Seniors - Family - Newborns	- What photographers do I know (ask for advice) - Find out the market range for each type of shoot - What makes me different - Define cost: camera body, lens, memory card, flash - What's my start date

Four Month Focus

Build Portfolio	Action
1. Research the best equipment for my budget.	1. Define Price List
2. Begin by taking photographs of friends and family for experience with less pressure	2. - Shadow/assist a professional photographer - Call and schedule a photoshoot for friends/family for examples
3. Shoot at a discount, for experience and footage	3. Build a portfolio

Goal #1

Example Page

Develop How

Internal Insight: *Photography comes naturally to me. I've always been interested in photography and it brings me joy. I have an artistic eye and love to shoot with a creative perspective.*

Genuine Growth: *Sign-up and take photography classes through Roberts Camera store or local college continuing education class. Get advice from a professional. Become better at what I already do.*

Notable Navigation: *Research how to build a business. Set a date to begin my LLC and plan details and create a timeline. Focus on one step at a time so it doesn't feel overwhelming*

Imaginative Ideas: *I'll be personally invested in my client's experience. Weddings: I'll ask about the proposal, Seniors: we'll talk about their dreams and future, with each type of shoot I'll find ways to bring those details into the shoot - make it memorable*

Transformative Truths: *I am skillful in photography. I have a natural ability. I will learn what I don't know and become better. There are opportunities and room for me as a photographer.*

Empowering Efforts: *I am the key to change in my life. I will work every day for 1 - 2 hours to become better and move forward as a photographer and entrepreneur.*

Goal # 1

Decide What _____

Define Why _____

Brainstorm Boxes

Four Month Focus

1. _____
   _____
   _____

2. _____
   _____
   _____

3. _____
   _____
   _____

Goal # 1

Develop How _____

Internal Insight _____
_____
_____

Genuine Growth _____
_____
_____

Notable Navigation _____
_____
_____

Imaginative Ideas _____
_____
_____

Transformative Truths _____
_____
_____

Empowering Efforts _____
_____
_____

Goal # 2

<u>Decide What</u>

<u>Define Why</u>

Brainstorm Boxes

Four Month Focus

1.

2.

3.

Goal # 2

Develop How _____

Internal Insight _____
_____
_____

Genuine Growth _____
_____
_____

Notable Navigation _____
_____
_____

Imaginative Ideas _____
_____
_____

Transformative Truths _____
_____
_____

Empowering Efforts _____
_____
_____

Goal # 3

Decide What _____

Define Why _____

Brainstorm Boxes

Four Month Focus

1. _____	
2. _____	
3. _____	

Goal # 3

Develop How

Internal Insight

Genuine Growth

Notable Navigation

Imaginative Ideas

Transformative Truths

Empowering Efforts

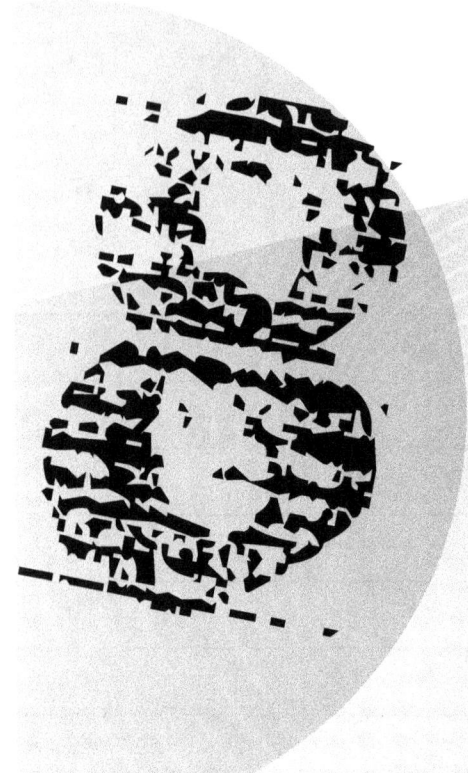

Grasping Growth

"To explore strange new worlds, to seek out new life and new civilizations to boldly go where no one has gone before." One day Gene Roddenberry, the creator of Star Trek, gave birth to this epic phrase. He allowed his imagination to flow and discovered a brand new plane of creative existence. Now, picture a pitch-black sky, absolute darkness fills the air, except for the vividly glowing moon surrounded by dazzling stars. A sky full of wonderment and possibility is stretched out above you.

It is normal for us to expect the beauty and grandeur of darkness to visit us nightly. And just like this natural occurrence, it is easy for our routine to become what we "expect" out of life. If we aren't careful, our lives can become predictable instead of venturing out into brave new territories. Think of the words "to go where no one has gone before" and imagine the boundless possibilities. What new worlds will await us? Are we willing to allow ourselves to inhabit our wildest dreams?

We have the ability to speak greatness into our lives and fully grasp the seemingly unimaginable. We can break away from our status quo and dream beyond our limitations in a new place of self-discovery. Then we can develop the potential planted within us.

Our imaginations color our creativity and mold our momentum. Once we can see the splendor of our potential, our excuses can disappear. It is up to us to realize the strength we possess and create opportunities to use it. We define our possibilities.

> What you are thinking of is what you are becoming.
> - Muhammad Ali

Growth requires movement, and I had to stop accepting my excuses for stagnant immobility. I viewed my constant busyness as action, which it was, but it had no true direction. I had gone from fulfilling one role to another instead of defining it. I was comfortable and caught in my routine, identifying myself by my tasks instead of my internal voice. And because I felt validated by the voices around me, instead of the voice within me, I had accepted the redundancy of my life.

Unknowingly, I believed that I was accomplishing my potential by gaining the approval of others. And as long as I felt relatively happy, I didn't see the need for change, so I continued wandering. I needed a way to look beyond my moments of mediocrity so that I could redefine my vantage point.

I didn't know that change was slowly brewing beneath the surface of my contentment. And this shift would cause my dormant dreams to awaken and demand my attention.

Life has caused me to look within myself and willfully pursue my definition of greatness. But first, I had to face my emotional insecurities and push myself past the pain, which then revealed my strength in the process. I fought against my distractions and resisted the temptation to become what others expected me to be. I then realized that the only person I need to impress is myself.

With deep soul exploration, we can peel away the surface of our commitments and dig into the depths of our desires. Will we accept the challenge of self-discovery, to ensure that the world isn't robbed of our unique existence?

What would happen if we counted ourselves worthy of our time and defined our ideal contribution to the world?

There are multiple methods to reach our goals. Our dreams don't have an expiration date or deadline, and as long as we work towards them, they will continue to live. Timelines can get stalled or derailed, and sometimes we have to be flexible and adjust for our misplaced moments. If we are determined to believe in ourselves, then we can continue to push forward after we have gotten off course.

The more we commit to our vision, it will begin to expand and take on a life of its own. Imagine the power possessed by our internal desire, picture it having a heartbeat and a voice, it wants to live, it wants to breathe. There is a consciousness within us that will help direct our path if we listen and react to the soul of who we are.

When we are confident in ourselves, we can realize our undeniable power. Then we can reposition our minds realizing that we are the force propelling our change. We are the validation of our voice as we grant ourselves permission to grow.

By thought, the thing you want is brought to you. By action, you receive it
- Wallace Wattles

Time To Define

1 What are the excuses that are allowing you to be stagnant?

2. If you could spend the rest of your life doing one thing, what would it be?

3. What time each day will you devote to your dream development?

NOTES
(Whispering Thoughts)

QUOTE

"To be a great champion, you must believe you are the best. If you're not, pretend you are."
– Muhammad Ali

Caged Warrior

Eager anticipation is coursing through their veins. No one will concede today because both contenders refuse to surrender. The battle will be relentless, and one of the opponents will be brought to their knees in defeat. In the past, they have each beaten their rivals with a sneer and mocking grin. They have each tasted victory and defeat, which has prepared them for this moment.

Imagine them now; their swollen shoulder muscles glisten with beads of sweat, and their jaws are firm with grimacing teeth. The wrinkles in their foreheads are intensified by the curve of their dark eyebrows. Their eyes are glaring deep into the other one's soul. As they pound their fists into their opposite glove, sweat glides down their chest as their muscles jump from the powerful force. They stalk the ring like dogs pacing back and forth, barking to intimidate a potential intruder. And they bait each other with boisterous claims, trying to instill fear. They know that only one of them will win, and the ultimate champion will be declared.

The bell rings, and they charge fearlessly towards their enemy, unwilling to miss the first punch. No hesitation or self-doubt can be seen from the outside. Their flawless precision is equally matched; they appear to be unfazed after simultaneous jabs. They follow-up with right hooks and uppercuts.

Drops of blood fly through the air. They know each other's strategy and next move as if it were instinct. The deeper they look into the other one's eyes, the illusion begins to fade away, and it's replaced by a mirror reflection. Suddenly the ring cannot be found, and the boxing match disappears as you come to yourself and realize that it was you, you were the one in the ring equally matched by your internal adversary. And the fight for dominance will be won when you realize the power you possess to control your reality. What matters most to you, and what are you willing to fight for?

Two versions of our existence live within us. When we are dedicated to discovering and living our dreams, then we can evolve. And when we know who we are, then we can control our narrative and direct our path.

Our decisions determine our future, and we get to define our lives. Unapologetically and without permission, seek the change that will cause you to grow. Honor your potential and validate your voice by believing in your greatness. You are the champion in your life, now live like it.

Now What?

For exciting opportunities to help you move forward visit:

www.melissaofficer.com

Notes

Notes

Notes

Notes

www.ingramcontent.com/pod-product-compliance
Lightning Source LLC
LaVergne TN
LVHW051527070426
835507LV00023B/3339